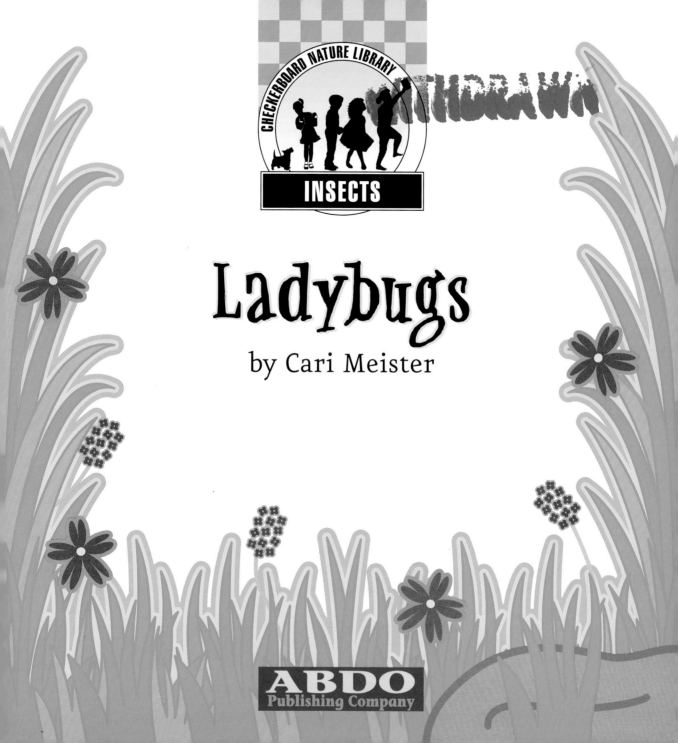

CHECKERBOARD NATURE LIBRARY

WITHDRAWN

INSECTS

Ladybugs

by Cari Meister

ABDO
Publishing Company

visit us at
www.abdopub.com

Published by ABDO Publishing Company, 4940 Viking Drive, Suite 622, Edina, Minnesota 55435. Copyright © 2001 Abdo Consulting Group, Inc., Pentagon Tower, P.O. Box 36036, Minneapolis, Minnesota 55435 USA. International copyrights reserved in all countries. No part of this book may be reproduced in any form without written permission from the publisher.

Printed in the United States

Illustrators: Edwin Beylerian, Carey Molter

Cover photo: John Foxx Images

Interior photos: Artville, Corel, Corbis Images, Digital Vision, John Foxx Imates, Peter Arnold, Inc., PhotoDisc, PictureQuest

Editors: Tamara L. Britton, Kate A. Furlong

Design and production: MacLean & Tuminelly

Library of Congress Cataloging-in-Publication Data

Meister, Cari.
   Ladybugs / Cari Meister.
       p. cm. -- (Insects)
   ISBN 1-57765-463-3
       1. Ladybugs--Juvenile literature. [1. Ladybugs.] I. Title.

QL596.C65 M45 2000
595.76'9--dc21

00-056884

Contents

What is a Ladybug?

If there is a ladybug in your garden, leave it be! Ladybugs eat pesky insects that destroy plants. Ladybugs are a gardener's best friend.

Most ladybugs are tiny. They come in different colors. Many of them are red. Some are yellow. Some are orange. Some ladybugs have spots. Some ladybugs have no markings at all.

There are many different kinds of ladybugs.

4

Ladybugs are sometimes called ladybird beetles. That is because a ladybug is a kind of beetle, just like a June bug or a firefly. Earth has more kinds of beetles than any other insect. It has more than 250,000 kinds of beetles. More than 4,500 kinds of beetles are ladybugs!

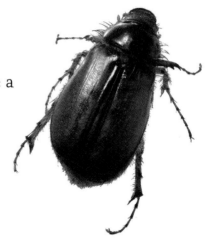

Ladybugs are beetles. June bugs, fireflies, and weevils are beetles, too.

A Ladybug's Body

Like all insects, ladybugs have three body sections. These three sections are the head, thorax, and abdomen. The first section is the head. Behind the head is the thorax. The abdomen is the final section. All three sections make up the body of an adult ladybug.

A ladybug's head has two short feelers. They are called antennae. The antennae sense things, like movement and smells. Adult ladybugs use their antennae to find each other when they are ready to mate. A ladybug's head also has eyes. And it has mouthparts to chew food.

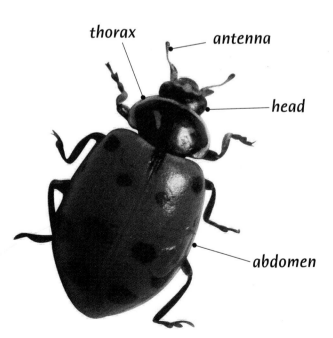

thorax

antenna

head

abdomen

A ladybug's thorax has six short, sturdy legs. The thorax also holds two sets of wings. The outer wings look like a hard, smooth shell. They are called elytra. Elytra protect a ladybug's inner wings, which are long and

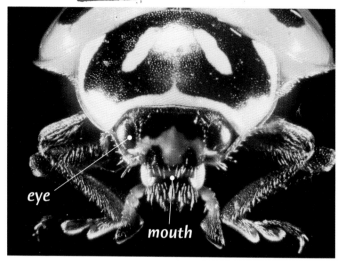

eye

mouth

inner wing

leg

outer wing (elytra)

thin. When a ladybug flies, the inner wings beat fast. The outer wings stabilize the flight. Ladybugs are not fast flyers. Most of the time they move by walking.

7

A ladybug's abdomen holds many of its organs. The organs have two main jobs. They must digest food and pump blood. The heart is like a tube. It's long and thin. The heart pumps blood throughout the ladybug's body. The digestive system also looks like a long, thin tube. It grinds up food. Most of a ladybug's food is digested in the gut.

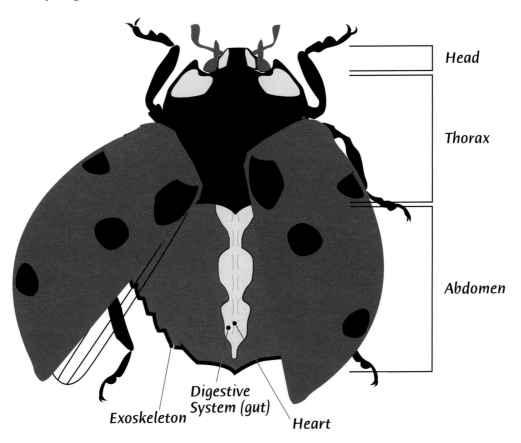

Head

Thorax

Abdomen

Exoskeleton

Digestive System (gut)

Heart

To protect its organs, a ladybug has a hard shell. It is called an exoskeleton. It keeps the organs from being crushed.

This ladybug's inner wings and elytra are easy to see.

How a Ladybug Grows

Young ladybugs look much different than adult ladybugs. This is because when ladybugs grow, they go through four different stages. These four stages are egg, larva, pupa, and adult.

Females lay eggs about one week after mating. The eggs are yellow. Ladybugs lay their eggs on leaves. The eggs don't fall off because they are sticky. In a few days, the eggs turn white. This means the larvae are ready to hatch.

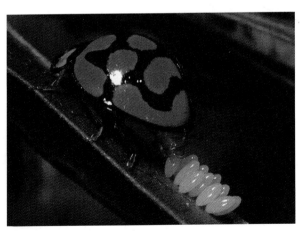

Female ladybug laying eggs on a leaf.

The larvae start out very small. They have tiny spikes on their body for protection. Ladybug larvae spend most of their time eating. Just like adult ladybugs, the larvae eat aphids. They eat so many aphids that their skin grows too small. Larvae shed their skin three times.

Next, the larva becomes pupa. It stops eating. It attaches itself to a leaf. It spends its time resting. Then, its skin peels open. A hard shell forms. Inside, a ladybug is forming.

After five days, an adult ladybug is ready to come out. It pulls itself out of its shell. At first its body is soft and wet. Soon it dries and hardens. Then, its color and spots begin to develop.

Ladybug larvae.

This ladybug just shed its pupa shell.

What a Ladybug Eats

Ladybugs are picky eaters. They only eat a few things. Ladybugs love to eat aphids. Aphids are small bugs that suck nutrients from plants. Aphids are pests. They can destroy entire gardens and orchards. Ladybugs are helpful insects because they eat pesky ones, like aphids.

Ladybug eating an aphid.

Aphids and scale insects are easy for ladybugs to catch. Aphids do not have any way to protect themselves. They can't run or fly away. All a ladybug has to do is walk up to an aphid and take a bite! It's a good thing aphids are so easy to catch. Ladybugs do not have strong legs to capture their prey.

A hungry ladybug can eat up to 60 aphids a day. Some larvae may eat 500 aphids in one day!

Ladybug larva eating aphids.

Where Ladybugs Live

Ladybugs live on all **continents** except Antarctica. They are common in the United States and Canada.

Ladybugs make their homes in places where they can find food. They live in **pastures**. They live in orchards. They also live in backyard gardens. Leaves and stems are a ladybug's favorite spots to live.

Ladybugs live in orchards and gardens.

When cold weather sets in, ladybugs find safe, warm places to rest. Ladybugs hibernate in large groups. They often hibernate under a pile of leaves, under rocks, or in a hollow tree.

Ladybugs on a rock in winter.

Enemies

Ladybugs have few enemies. Sometimes ants, spiders, and birds will eat ladybugs. But this does not happen often. Most insects and birds stay away from ladybugs.

A ladybug has many ways to protect itself. For example, it can squirt yellow liquid from its leg joints. The liquid is actually blood. It smells and tastes bad. This keeps predators away.

A spider eating a ladybug caught in its web.

16

A ladybug's smooth, round body also protects it. This shape is hard for an enemy to attack. Some scientists believe that the bright colors on a ladybug's wings keep predators away, too.

A ladybug's round body and bright colors help protect it from enemies.

Ladybugs & People

Most ladybugs are helpful. They eat other harmful insects. Farmers and gardeners have been using ladybugs for a long time. In 1888, scale insects covered many orange groves in California. The scale insects sucked nutrients out of the trees. The trees almost died. Farmers released millions of ladybugs in the groves. The ladybugs ate the scale insects and saved the trees.

An orange grower inspects his crops.

Today, there are people who harvest ladybugs. They call themselves "buggers." Buggers go into woods and meadows to collect ladybugs. They collect ladybugs that are hibernating. Buggers ship their ladybugs to orchards and gardens.

Not all ladybugs are helpful. Some ladybugs do not eat insects. Some ladybugs just eat plant leaves.

A bugger fills a bag with ladybugs.

This girl is putting ladybugs on the roses to eat harmful insects.

Fun Facts

- Ladybugs clean their faces with their front legs after they eat.

- A ladybug's **elytra** get darker as it ages.

🐞 It takes about 3,000 ladybugs to protect an acre of land from plant-eating insects.

🐞 Beetles have been around for over 200 million years.

🐞 Ladybugs were once thought to have magical powers.

Glossary

continent – one of the seven great land masses on Earth. The seven continents are North America, South America, Europe, Africa, Asia, Australia, and Antarctica.

elytra – a ladybug's hard outer wings that protect the soft inner wings.

exoskeleton – the outer casing that protects an insect.

hibernate – a period of time when an insect is resting, usually during colder weather.

larva – the stage of an insect's life that comes between hatching and pupa.

nutrients – important things, like vitamins, that all living things need to survive.

pasture – a grassy field of hillside.

predator – an animal that eats and or kills other animals.

pupa – the stage in an insect's life that comes between larva and adult.

prey – animals that are eaten by predators.

stabilize – to make something steady and firm.

Web Sites

http://www.ex.ac.uk/bugclub/
Join the Bug Club! This site for young entomologists includes a newsletter, puzzles, and games.

http://www.insecta.com
This site, hosted by the University of British Columbia, has great information on all kinds of bugs. Read about the bug of the month, listen to great bug sounds, and look at a bug family tree!

http://www.schoolnet.ca/vp-pv/ladybug/e/ladybuge/index.htm
Have you found a ladybug but aren't sure what kind it is? Come to the Canadian Nature Federation's web to find out!

These sites are subject to change. Go to your favorite search engine and type in ladybugs for more sites.

Index